SHIRLEY GREE

ANIMAL HOMES

WATER

photographs by Oxford Scientific Films

Newington Press

First published in the
United States in 1991 by
Newington Press
2 Old New Milford Road
Brookfield, Connecticut 06804

First published in Great Britain
in 1990 by Belitha Press Limited

Library of Congress Cataloging-in-Publication Data
Greenway, Shirley
Animal homes: water/Shirley Greenway;
photographs by Oxford Scientific Films.
Brookfield, Conn.: Newington Press, 1991.
24 p.: col. ill.; 21 cm (Animal homes)
Shows which aquatic animals live in different
kinds of water—seas, lakes, rivers, and ponds—
and how they breed.
1. Aquatic animals—Juvenile literature.
2. Animals—Habitations—Juvenile literature
I. Oxford Scientific Films.   II. Title.   III. Series.
ISBN: 1-878137-10-7   591.52642

Words in **bold** are explained in the glossary at
the end of this book.

In the watery world of seas, lakes, rivers, and ponds there live an astonishing number of animals—from the largest animals in the world to tiny creatures so small you cannot see them. Animals live in all kinds of water—in salt water and fresh water, in icy cold northern oceans and warm **tropical** seas, in fast-moving rivers and **stagnant** reed-filled ponds.

One water animal is the lesser-spotted dogfish (left), which is really a small shark. It has a peculiar purse-like egg case in which a young dogfish grows (above). Attached to a handy water weed the **translucent** case is the perfect protection for the baby shark until it is ready to come out.

3

Most frogs raise their young in water. The females lay clusters of round eggs, in puddles and ponds, which hatch into tiny tadpoles. Frog tadpoles are very good at finding food, and they grow very fast. At their earliest stage they are just a large big-mouthed head and a long thin tail—neither fish nor frog! The tadpoles go on eating and growing, and soon their legs appear. When at last their fish-like **gills** have been replaced by lungs, their tails disappear and they are ready to leave the pond. But they never stray too far from water, and cold weather brings them back to **hibernate** in the soft mud at the bottom.

4

Many birds make their homes on water. Grebes live on ponds, lakes, and marshes all over the world. The little grebe builds a large floating nest of water plants in which to lay its eggs. The chicks hatch one at a time and clamber on to their mother's back. They cling on tightly even when the adult dives. With their spindly legs set far back on their bodies, grebes are really at home only on water, and prefer swimming to flying! Underwater they are quick, agile, and silent as they hunt for insects and small fishes.

African pike live in the great flooded plain created each year when the waters of the Okavango River rise. They hunt among the flooded grasslands waiting in ambush for their **prey.** When it comes near, the pike attacks—catching it with a snap of its sharp-toothed jaws.

When they are ready to breed, the pike choose a protected spot among the dense water reeds. Here they build a meringue-like nest of foam on the surface of the water. The

female lays her eggs below, and they float upward into the sticky bubbles. The foam protects the eggs and keeps them moist until they are ready to hatch.

After the young pike hatch, they remain at the nest, hanging by threads from the foam. They eat the remains of the egg yolk—growing bigger and stronger. Both parents guard the nest, adding more foam, until the **hatchlings** are old enough to swim away and hunt for food.

Another father who looks after his young is the male seahorse. This beautiful animal is an odd-looking fish that lives among underwater grasses and seaweed. It swims upright with the help of a rapidly moving fin on its back. The male has a special opening on its underside called a "brood pouch." At **spawning** time the female seahorse fills the pouch with eggs, and the male carries the growing babies inside him for up to six weeks. When the tiny seahorses come out of the pouch they are fully formed miniature versions of their parents and able to swim immediately.

Sea anemones cluster on sea-washed rocky shores or on sandy seabeds all over the world. These beautifully colored creatures may look like an underwater garden of bright flowers. But in fact they are animals, each equipped with dangerous stinging cells with which they catch **prey.** As the tide washes over them, anemones unfurl their waving **tentacles**, searching the water for food. If an unwary shrimp or a small fish comes near, it is killed by the anemone's barbed cells—like little "arrows"—and eaten.

Anemones may spend their lives attached to a single rock, or they may release themselves and move to another rock or clump of seaweed. Sometimes one anemone will sting a smaller one that comes too close. Red anemones usually win these battles for space! The young grow from **fertilized** eggs inside the female. Then, when they are fully developed, they burst out of her mouth and float away—perfect tiny anemones, complete with stings.

American alligators build large nest mounds on river-banks in which to raise their eggs. The mother covers the mound with leaves and branches to keep the eggs warm. She protects her eggs fiercely until they are ready to hatch.

After three months the young break through the leathery shells and call loudly to their mother to set them free. She carries them gently to a "nursery pool," where they stay until they are old enough to move into deeper water. The **hatchlings** spend a year or more with their mother—often playing up and down her long scaly body—while they, too, grow into fearsome-looking adults!

With its strong back flippers, short front paws, and thick, warm fur, the sea otter is entirely at home in the cold waters of the North Pacific. It spends most of its time in the sheltered coastal waters, playing among the rocks. It dives to the seabed to search for crabs, sea urchins, and shellfish, which it brings to the surface to eat. Floating lazily along on its back, the clever sea otter sometimes uses a flat stone to break the hard shells of

shellfish. At other times, its long flat body makes a perfect table from which to nibble a fist-sized fish.

A sea otter can even sleep afloat, wrapping its body in handy fronds of seaweed to keep itself from floating away while it dozes. The female otter comes up on to the rocks once a year to give birth to a single pup. Mother and child soon go back into the sea, where the pup soon finds that the gently moving waves make a perfect cradle.

Seafarers' tales are full of strange creatures such as mermaids. But those half-human, half-fish wonders may well have been no more than sleek young manatees with their smooth, pale bodies, strong fishlike tails, and small, bright eyes. The huge old adults are heavy and wrinkled, with bristly snouts.

The rare manatee is a sea-living **mammal** that spends its life in shallow coastal waters. It feeds on water plants and pops up to the surface now and then to take a breath of air. The fast-growing calves go on nursing until they are almost as large as their patient mothers.

Hippopotamuses like to live together. More than a hundred adults and their young may rest on a sandbar in the evening sunlight. The hippo's name means "river horse," and it leads its life half on land and half in water. Because they lose so much water through their smooth skins, hippos spend the warm daylight hours beneath the surface of a sluggish river or lake—only their eyes, ears, and nostrils can be seen above the water. They can sink their huge bulk

fully beneath the water and remain there for up to five minutes, calmly walking along the river bottom. At night hippos follow well-known paths to their favorite **grazing** grounds.

The female hippos leave the herd to give birth to their babies—occasionally underwater. The tiny new hippo swims quickly to the surface to take its first breath. When it is time to return to the herd, the mother keeps the baby very close to her, teaching it the ways of the river.

Humpback whales are very playful for such huge and heavy animals. The largest creatures that ever lived on Earth, whales are **mammals** that live entirely in the sea. Their **streamlined** shapes are made for swimming, and their great weight is supported by the water. They can leap and dive and play. Humpback males and females often slap each other with their huge white flippers—gentle pats that echo for great distances.

Every two or three years, a female humpback gives birth to a single calf. Born underwater, the baby whale swims quickly to the surface to take its first breath. To breathe, a whale opens its "blowhole," blows out old air, and takes in a fresh breath before diving again. The humpback mother nurses her calf for a whole year. She protects and guides it as they swim together, their flippers glowing in the underwater gloom.

Index/Glossary

alligators 15
anemone 13

birds 7

egg case 3

fertilized able to develop and grow 13
fish 3, 8, 11
frogs 4

gills the part of the body underwater-living animals use for breathing 4
grazing eating growing plants 21
grebe 7

hatchling an animal, such as a fish or bird, just out of the egg 9, 15
hibernate to spend winter keeping very still while food is scarce 4
hippopotamus 20–21

lesser-spotted dogfish 3

mammal a warm-blooded, furry or hairy animal that can feed its young with its own milk 18, 22
manatee 18

pike, African 8–9
prey an animal that is killed and eaten by another animal 8, 12

sea anemones 12–13
seahorse 11
sea otter 16–17
shark 3
spawning laying eggs, especially said of fish or frogs 11
stagnant water that isn't flowing 3
streamlined being a good shape for going easily through air or water 22

tadpoles 4
tentacles long armlike parts of the bodies of some animals 12
translucent letting light through 3
tropical belonging to the hot areas of the world 3

whales 22–3

Photo Credits
The publishers wish to thank the following for permission to reproduce copyright material: **Oxford Scientific Films** for front cover (Kim Westerskor); title page (David Wrigglesworth); pp 2, 3, 4, 12 and 13 (G. I. Bernard); p 5 (Stephen Dalton); p 6 (D.J. Saunders); p 7 (George Bernard); p 8 (Carol Farneti); p 9 (Partridge Films—Karen Ross); p 10 (Kathie Atkinson); p 11 (Animals Animals—Zig Leszczynski); p 14 (James Robinson); p 15 (Stan Osolinski); p 16 and back cover (Animals Animals—Lewis Trusty); p 17 (Lon E. Lauber); p 18 (Animals Animals—Clyde Lockerwood); p 19 (Animals Animals—W. Gregory Brown); p 20 (Anthony Bannister); p 21 (Tom Leach); p 22 (Tony Martin); p 23 (Planet Earth Pictures—Rosemary Chastney).